Duct Tape Won't Fix This

A father's perspective

on raising a child

with a chronic illness

Duct Tape Won't Fix This is a work of non-fiction, a personal reflection of one man's journey.

Published in the United States
by Riverhaven Books,
www.RiverhavenBooks.com

ISBN: 978-1-937588-42-7

Printed in the United States of America
by Country Press, Lakeville, Massachusetts
Edited and designed by Stephanie Lynn Blackman
Whitman, Massachusetts

I would like to take a moment to mention those who have lent me support and advice over the years:

Soul Quest Men's Council, my brothers;

WIW Plymouth and Hyannis;

Christy and Ted;

Lee, Bev, Sharon – the ladies at P. P. L.;

Kerry Cudmore;

Janine Covequeen Sullivan;

Julie Kembel;

Maureen O'Brien;

Tom and Reiko @ TRB Designs;

and all those who have cheered me on.

Join the conversation at
www.ducttapewontfixthis.com
www.themagichatproject.com

And find us on Facebook at
Duct Tape Won't Fix This
The Magic Hat Project

Forward

In 1969, after dating my girlfriend for a couple of years, we got married. After we settled into our apartment, we started saving for a house. We worked for a year saving a down payment. We both worked and we banked her pay for a year, or was it mine? Whatever. At the end of a year we had a down payment saved and bought a house. That was 1970.

We were cruising along, following the American dream and it seemed we were on target. It took a year to bring the house up to our standards. Then in 1971 we got pregnant and started our family. We were in fact humming along, thinking we were on track like everyone else. Three years later our second child was born and we were now the average American family: mom, dad, two kids, a dog, and a house with a mortgage. Life was normal for three years and we raised the kids with all the birthday parties and holiday events, growing to know their cousins, aunts, uncles, and extended family. Then, in the third year of my youngest child's life, a new story began. A story no one wants to read, never mind live through.

So why am I deciding to live through this story again?

I have to ask myself, what is my long-term vision for this project? My first thought when trying to answer that question is, who am I to have a vision? The real question should be who am I to present this information and *not* have a well-defined vision to help those who are looking at this for the very first time. I do have a vision, and this is it:

1. This book opens the door to meaningful conversation. This topic covers a problem that thirty-two million men deal with on a daily basis and there is no help offered to them. We need to work together, lean on each other, and help each other figure it out.

2. By addressing this topic we salvage marriages and

families. How many women and children have ever even thought that we are actually affected by this in a very profound way?

3. Coming together shows that we are strong and care about our families. By doing this we become part of a larger family, the thirty-two million dads currently dealing with this situation alone. Can you imagine the clout we could muster in the medical community if we spoke as one voice?

4. Creating communities of men around the country where we come together to speak our truths and are understood where we are at that exact moment by others who know at an instinctual level because we are living it, first-hand, present tense or have experienced it.

5. I want what we are doing here to be the example for other men around the country to come together and start addressing their passions. The environment, the homeless, the thing that ignites their passion, whatever that passion is. We need to take back the responsibility of fixing these problems and stop waiting for someone else to do it.

6. I want men to plant a foot and say it stops with me. Families have always been the foundation of this country. With the divorce rates as high as they are, we need to fix what is broken in our families first. We need to be the example by setting the bar high and not accepting any less.

7. Teach men to be selfish. My meaning is different than the usual one. What I suggest is to be selfish in a way that refreshes you so that you are capable of giving to and supporting those you love.

8. Come together in community and not competition. We need to fix this problem, this town, this state, and this country. We are the answer to this question.

9. That this information unites us so that we can be available to and for each other. Circumstances tend to isolate us, but now we have a flag to rally around and the option to choose

a new course of action.

10. Ultimately, we need to ask ourselves different questions. Instead of laying blame and pointing fingers, we need to ask, what is my part in this situation? No small question. If we are looking to make the changes suggested here, then we cannot ask the same old questions. We need to take that leap of faith that if we lead, others will follow. I have seen proof of that in the men's group I have belonged to for twenty-six years.

The following is my take on the story…

How It Started

This story begins in 1976: before computers, cell phones, iPads, iPods, and a partridge in a pear tree.

My daughter was three years old and complaining of an achy bum, stiff joints, and was lethargic. Off to the doctor for a check-up with my wife and her mother. Our pediatrician was off that day so they saw his fill-in who for some reason decided to proceed by ordering blood work.

When he saw what was going on he admitted her to the hospital saying she had pneumonia. He knew it was something bad, but he was not going to be the one who broke the news. Our doctor was due back the following day, so he could have the honor.

That night, on my way home from work, when I heard that my baby was in the hospital, I immediately went to visit her. It was after visiting hours but they let me in. As if they could keep me out! I still believed that she only had pneumonia and would be home in the morning.

The next day my wife and her mom went to fetch my daughter. The doctor pulled my wife aside and told her that she needed to bring our daughter into the city to have some more extensive tests done, tests that he did not have the ability to do in his office.

I got the call at work and left immediately. The ride in was small talk, but the anxiety and confusion could have been cut with a knife. My head was spinning. I wasn't sure exactly where the hospital was but I knew it is in a seedy part of the city. We got there and found a parking spot, found the building, the old part of this hospital, and went in.

We went up a few floors and then we had to go up a ramp to get to the appropriate floor in the attached building. The two buildings were half a floor off in height which is why the ramp and not stairs. I knew that up that ramp was the cancer ward. *THE CANCER WARD.*

I thought one thing: This cannot be happening, not to my child. This only happens to others. How could this even be a remote possibility? Did I do something wrong in another life? How do I lead us onward?

I was so over my head that the only thing I could do was to keep us moving forward. I didn't want to go up that ramp but up we went.

At the top there was a waiting area with a couch and a few chairs and a couple of plastic plants with no windows; it was very dark and foreboding. Then there were those swinging doors we had to go through.

My mind was in a fog. I bargained with God to get the test and have it be something else so we could go home. We were not supposed to be there.

All the while I was trying to put up a strong façade for my family. That was my belief at the time; dad is supposed to fix things so I needed to be brave in order to keep the women and children safe at all costs.

Through those doors we entered the ward. Without realizing it, I walked us into a nightmare situation that I had no ability to control or comprehend. The sound of crying children mixed with that of crying adults, the smell of fear, that hospital hygienic cleaner mixed with urine. Or was it the salty tears or just my fear recycling itself through my nostrils?

The parents all had that thousand-yard empty stare.

God, get us out of here.

We had to sign in and take a seat. This has to be every

parent's worst nightmare. After sitting for what seemed an eternity, watching the other parents with their own sick babies trying to comfort and console their children and each other, the stress was ratcheting up by the moment.

I for one was ready to explode, wanting the test to get done so we could find out that it is something else and could go home.

Finally, it was our turn.

Do we go with her or stay here?

Will she be all right?

"Don't worry, hon. We are right here when you are done."

They took our tiny child down the hall and into a room. They did not go far enough down the hall; we could hear our baby screaming. I looked at my wife and she looked at me and the only thing I could do was move us away from the sound that I was helpless to prevent.

That look of fear on my wife's face, the haunting scream from my baby, the ward full of fear and bewilderment, the sense that there was no hope, the resorting back to primal fear, fight or flight, being totally unable to reconcile what was going on and what lay ahead, trying to understand my part in what was about to happen.

Knowing in my heart one thing: that it was my job to fix this any way I could.

Where do I find the answers I need to make this right?

All this and more flashed through my mind in a millisecond and just kept circling around in my head. The only thing that came to me was do not show any fear. Be in control and show no fear.

The one and only feeling present in this situation and I needed to stifle it for the good of the family. If I faltered, it would all fall apart; or was it I would fall apart?

That place at the top of the ramp gave us enough distance to not hear my baby screaming.

At the same time it was hard to even look at my wife and try to comprehend what the fear was doing to her. I could see it in her face, or was that the reflection of my face? My mind races back into my past trying to assimilate the feelings with anything I may have felt before. NOTHING. The only things that came up were the stories of my father's generation. Do it for mom, sis, apple pie, and country. Take nothing for yourself. It is all about them. *You* are responsible.

We never discussed it, but it was nonverbally understood that the child came first and we were responsible. It appeared we fell into our own survival modes. That place where we knew that it was all or nothing to keep our child alive. Nothing else mattered. The only way I could cope was to hunker down, just try to keep it moving forward.

I would love to tell you that at this time and in this place I rose to the occasion and did the superhuman thing that made for the usual happy ending. Perhaps this is where the feeling of inadequacy came from.

I, as dad, did not have the answers. I did not even have the questions. My new load to carry: self-doubt, hopelessness, and any other adjectives that describe fault.

What I do know is that when it is your child in distress, you shift into hyper-drive to figure out how to fix it. You look into anything you can find that remotely describes her symptoms.

Having done that, I found that just made it worse. Some stuff just did not apply to her disease and symptoms and were in fact worse than what she had.

Be careful how you approach this information gathering so as not to add undue pressure on yourself. Unfortunately, or perhaps fortunately, there was not an abundance of information available at that time. I am not sure I could have handled the truth or options as they pertained to my child. I had to progress as though it would be all right if I kept us moving forward. That was my only salvation or belief that kept me going.

This was the first time, at the top of that ramp, I felt totally helpless to protect my family. Little did I know it was not going to be the last.

Who Am I?

I am not a doctor, therapist, or health professional of any type. What you read here is my take on my situation that has gone on for thirty-six years. Have I done therapy? Yes. Do I suggest it? That is up to you. What I am suggesting here is that we begin a *conversation* among men in similar circumstances.

Will everyone participate? We will see. What my experience says is that a few will start and others will monitor the conversation to see if it is safe and, when that is proven, will join in.

I cannot fix you. You cannot fix me. What I believe is we can make a safe place for dads who have this kind of stress to come for some first-rate help from those who have gone down the path ahead of them and are willing to share their common experience.

Even if we just create a place to vent our frustrations, that is miles ahead of where we are now. I truly believe we can do so much more than that.

I know that I felt unique. That no one knew my pain. There are thirty-two million dads with chronically ill kids. How unique could I have been? What I did was buy into the BS that was slung and thus created more pain and suffering for myself. Do not do that.

We have been sold a bag of lies. Advertising gurus taught us that male role models such as the Marlboro Man and John Wayne were tough and silent and talked with their fists. We bought into that based on the feedback we got from our sources on how we should live: through television, radio, newspapers, and movies. This turns out to be more propaganda than factual information.

Still we tend toward the propaganda apparently, so we do not have to think for ourselves and go against what is cool.

At some point we need to take back our reality and quit living someone else's. Following someone else's idea of how we should be has caused us as men to suffer a great deal more than necessary.

Perhaps this is where I need you to trust my experience. I have been involved in a men's group for twenty-six years. We came together from varying backgrounds. What matters most is someone had the idea and was able to articulate it well enough that a bunch of us said, "Yeah, that sounds right."

We came together as men from differing backgrounds and life experiences with the idea that we would show up consistently, share our truth, and be as honest as we could. This was a totally new experience for us all.

We agreed to share the leadership of the group so we could gain the most by hearing opposing perspectives of life experiences. In the beginning it was difficult to share at this level, but we kept showing up and over the years were able to share from our souls, creating a level of trust.

Today there are eight men I would lay my life on the line for. As we worked, our ability to open up and share our truth started to show and other men wanted what we had and joined the group.

What I am trying to convey here is that when we as men come together with a purpose, we can change the world, or at least our corner of it.

The other thing I want to say here is that even with this level of trust where no topic is taboo, it still has not allowed me to get in touch with that pain that lives deep inside me. Only through talking with other men who have felt the pain at that same level will I be able to speak to mine and feel heard.

To have carried this burden alone for all those years has cost me large chunks of my life that I will never get back.

So how do I make sense of this? By reaching out to you, the dads, who may be able to gain from my story. Perhaps I can live vicariously through you. Truthfully, when and what I do for others is what makes me whole.

If after participating for a period of time you are not satisfied that what we are doing is helping, we offer a double your misery back refund with no questions asked. No time limit and we will pay the postage both ways.

BUT WAIT! THERE'S MORE!

We will even double that offer to quadruple your refund of misery with no questions asked. But you must act now. Okay, okay. It can't all be serious.

My Hope

This is *my* story. It is about my journey with my child who has had cancer six times over the last thirty-six years. I am not trying to tell your story, but I am willing to bet that once you boil away the circumstances our stories are more alike than they are different.

There will be differences between our religious beliefs, schooling, families of origin, and traditions. But when we analyze the core issues, they are exactly the same across all nationalities and self-imposed differences. So I ask you to proceed with an open mind. Help me to make a difference in families across this nation, possibly across the world but most especially in yours and mine.

Where and how do I begin to tell the story of my experiences as it pertains to my family? You and I are both the sum of our life experiences, good and bad. The way the universe has acted in my life has been through medical experiences from an early age. When I was one year old my sister died right after birth, at age eight my brother was born with a bad heart, at sixteen I was involved in a car wreck that left me broken from head to toe. Then I got my family started and my youngest daughter was diagnosed with Leukemia at age three; in the middle of that my older daughter needed surgery for Scoliosis.

What you do with the hand you have been dealt becomes your legacy. How did you act in the circumstances you were handed? Is anyone ever ready for what comes up, especially if it is less than pleasant? My guess is, probably not. So how do you adapt to these new issues as they present themselves.

I wish the following story was an introduction in how to live your life without any problems but it is not. What it is, however, is a look back over thirty-six years of trying, failing, trying something else. Persistence is the word that comes to mind for me here. If nothing else I was persistent in trying to find the answers to save my child and family.

I lived with a range of only four emotions at the time – happy, sad, depression, and rage. I sucked at caring for myself but that is one of the lessons this story is trying to impart. Balance has never been a part of my life story. Another important word to learn as it pertains to you and your life as well.

Going from being a responsible person in life and death situations for more than half of my life to being relegated to that old man who is tolerated and not needed or not thought of as having any knowledge that is pertinent in today's arena is a long and hard fall.

So these circumstances beg the question what now? Do I play that part or do I rear up and try to share my experiences with others and make a difference in the world outside my family?

By outside my family I mean all the families that are dealing with chronic illness. My hope is that by sharing a father's perspective, a new understanding will arise that will benefit the family unit as a whole. A large piece of my story follows and you get to be the judge. Hopefully, not being emotionally involved will help you transition through the information provided and you will be able to use it for your family where you are most certainly emotionally involved. Let's see where this takes us...

A Beginning

I had no idea how hard it was going to be to actually write this book. I knew it would change lives, including my own. Do I write it from a particularly negative perspective with all the raw emotions and anger that went with the experience or do I try to look at it as a cathartic experience for others as well as myself?

This story represents more than half of my life. If I try to say that there was no anger, resentment, depression, or a whole list of raw emotions, I would be lying. Hopefully, with all this time "in" I can do us both justice in telling this story with a balance between neutral complacency and open, hostile rage.

Announcing that I was going to write this book about being the father of a chronically ill child over the last thirty-six years sounded wonderful and noble to my ears and others as they cheered me on to do it. Then I had to decide, how deep am I willing to go?

If this writing is to be helpful or hopeful to you and me, then I feel obligated to tell the whole truth and that scares the heck out of me.

By my reliving that period of time, I believe, you will understand my truth. Do I have a clue and should you listen to what I say and should you add your voice? If I do not tell my truth, how can I ask you to? There is a line that must be adhered to and if I lose my balance in relating the facts it will become meaningless.

I intend to be painfully honest about my experience in hopes of engaging this particular population, *YOU*, the dads. I sat down and started taking notes about what actually transpired in certain situations and, low and behold, my demons were back, challenging me: Who do you think you are?

Fear, depression, guessing, looking back at the decisions I made and how they affected my family, having no one to talk to, friends and family walking out of my life, having someone find out how much I didn't know, being criticized, shame. Someone has to open this door and shine some light on what is not going on for one half of the partners in families in a crisis situation.

I almost talked myself out of writing this damn book.

After much inner searching and wrestling with my inner critic I have come to the place that I am comfortable enough in my own skin to tackle this project. Maybe you aren't there yet, and maybe after reading this you'll decide I'm not there either. However once you hear my side of the story and observe my raw emotions, I genuinely feel that you will understand and will be able to relate.

I have searched for help over a very long period of time and I can tell you with a high degree of certainty that there are no help programs for dads of chronically ill children anywhere in the country.

Prepare yourselves for the large and loud outcry from all the major hospitals and health centers claiming that they do that, it is under "Families". When I asked these institutions how many men were actually in these programs, I got the medical two-step. Dodgy stories of classified information and HIPPA compliance. Notice I didn't ask for names or any identifying information, just how *many* dads were taking advantage of their program.

Sounds to me like someone does not want to talk about what is truly lacking and their part in it. I did find one program in my area at one of the biggest and best, you would know the name, so I asked how it worked. I was told it was a voluntary drop-in on the first Tuesday of the month. I asked how many were involved and who ran it. I was told that the how many information was not available but when someone showed up the physical therapist came in to run the meeting. I asked if he had a sick child and was told he did not but he has "training". This is where my anger starts to raise its head but I am trying to be nice. That probably won't last.

The only letters you will find behind my name are Jr. I was named after my dad. The one person I wanted to be the exact opposite of as I moved through my life. My parents lost a child that was born after I was, and then had two daughters and another son who had a bad heart. My dad and I both had a sick child to deal with, both with a life-challenging disease, but he chose to crawl into a bottle: the summation of his experience of the war and not talking about it. Except for the bottle, I fell in line and picked up many of his bad habits.

This is where it starts to feel less than comfortable. I am asking men to come to a communal discussion when there has never been one that addresses these issues. No one has ever presented a forum around discussing the issues that are tearing our families apart. It did mine and the numbers speak for themselves: a huge divorce rate in families with sick children.

What I am offering is a place for us to come together in conversation only. Just to talk to each other. I am so tired of being alone and thinking that no one else knows what I am experiencing.

According to my research, there are thirty-two million dads with a chronically ill child in America right now. Could it possibly be that I am unique in feeling this way? I doubt it. I am not that important or different. Even if you are fortunate enough to have a loving woman around, what does she know about being a man? Her experience is totally different than that of a male. As far as they know all we do is talk sports, politics, fishing, hunting, cars, drinking, and *sex*. I tried to make that a four-letter word but spell check thwarted me.

I don't mean to make light of how difficult it is for us to ask for anything for ourselves. It is almost too painful to say, "I don't know" or "I need help" or "I can't do this." In this case I am the one who is asking for your help. Help me make sense of my thirty-six years of doing it. How can I fix my problem?

Use me as the one who needs this information. All I ask is that you state your truth, always. The theory here is I have your back and you have mine. What we say stays confidential so we can speak our truth and not fear it coming back on us. Without that we have nothing.

After you read my story I think you will have a pretty good idea of what worked and what didn't, how alone I felt, how much of life I guessed at, the things I wish I had a do-over for.

What I hope for is that something I say will resonate in you and inspire you to get your voice into the conversation. I need you. I hope you need me.

I fully expect this conversation to begin because there are thirty-two million of us with a chronically ill child at this writing. With no help in the foreseeable future from the medical establishment, we need to act now, for our families.

If statistics are to be used, more knowledgeable people than myself tell me that the divorce rate in families with sick kids is in the eighty-plus percent range. Not hard to buy into when it is fifty-fifty going in with no crisis.

So begins the story. It is not for the faint of heart. What I say actually happened and how I felt about it is true to the best of my ability. So put your seats in the upright position, close the tray tables, and buckle up; the vomit bags are in the pouch in front of you. We are taxiing out for takeoff.

Diagnosis

Finally, she was back in mom's arms. We were told, "Go sit and wait for the lab results."

Hours passed and finally the labs were back.

"Come into this room," they said.

Along with my family there were two nurses and an older female doctor with a heavy German accent.

Before I finish that thought, I need to set the stage about my beliefs related to cancer at that time. I believed two scenarios were the only outcomes available if you were diagnosed with cancer. If you got cancer, you died in six months or less *OR* if they opened you up surgically and exposed it to air, they sewed you up, sent you home and cut the time in half.

Those were my beliefs at that moment in time. Tell me, am I unique? Did any other father feel or believe differently when they learned about their child's illness? This is where I need to hear from you. In thirty-six years I have never had a meaningful conversation with another dad in my position thereby causing me to feel unique and alone. We don't talk. I have come to understand that I am just not that special, are you?

Back to the room. Diagnosis: your child has blood cancer, A.L.L., acute lymphocytic leukemia.

What I heard was your child is going to die before you.

Logic left the room and my life. So much more happened in that room that day. Receiving that news, for me, was like being hit in the chest with a Howitzer at point blank range. All air left my lungs. I could not breathe. I could not focus on what was just said; I was struggling to understand it all.

I feared for my family, I feared for myself. How was I going to make this okay? I looked at my wife and saw an empty look and that added to my desperation.

How was I as father, husband going to protect them and get us through what I believed was about to come?

I was still trying to grasp what had just happened. Four words changed my life in an instant.

What do I do? How do I move us forward? Where are we going? How can I beat the odds?

I was still trying to grasp a mouthful of air. After what seemed an eternity I was able to form the only question I could, "How long?"

Before we go on I need to ramble a bit here. As husband and dad I am supposed to protect my family from all bad things. Seeing my three-year-old cuddled up in her mom's lap shaking and whimpering, paired with my wife's distant stare, my mind was racing; I knew because I heard it pounding in my ears.

Everything I knew told me we were fucked and yet I was compelled to move us forward no matter what. Forward motion was the only answer I could wrap my mind around. I was shutting down emotionally. I could not allow myself to feel for if I did, I was done.

Back to the room again. As God is my judge, that doctor laughed and said, "Oh no, it's not like that anymore." She just told me my kid had cancer, which I believed was a death sentence and she laughed.

A very, very short time later she was removed from our case (never before or since then have I wanted to kill a woman with my bare hands).

The diagnosis had me on the ropes; I had no words or experience to propel us forward. Hell, I had no idea how to move myself forward, never mind my entire family.

Apparently I was not able to contain my outrage at that doctor who just laughed while giving me what I perceived was a death sentence for my child.

A very short time later the head of the department came out and took our case. She talked us through my anger and helped us get a handle on what was said in that room. We became friends and I believe she was instrumental in saving my child.

Her manner was straight out from the get-go. She told us that they were having great success with my child's type of leukemia and she would do everything she could to keep her with us. We were in for a bumpy ride in the beginning but we would get past that to a smoother ride in time.

She was not only the head of the department but was in the labs out back researching new medicines and was on the cutting edge as it pertained to us. About five years into treatment she transferred to another hospital. We followed her there as it was still within driving distance.

She saved my kid; no way did I trust anyone else with her care. This was very early in the process and I was in awe of the doctors.

As we moved forward I came to understand that they were mere mortals with a better education. They each brought their own personalities and bedside manner, or lack thereof, to their practice of medicine. Some actually had a sense of humor.

Yes, I needed to trust them with the care of my child but I needed to stand up for my child as well. Never be afraid to challenge a doctor if he or she is aloof, gruff, or just rubs you the wrong way; get another one or get another opinion. Some of them feel and treat you like they are gods. They are not. You already have enough on your plate and have no time or need to put up with that stuff. The most important thing is your child and your ability to communicate with that doctor at a level you can understand. It is in the best interest of your child. Screw the doctors' egos.

Traditionally, a hospital stay is required to begin chemotherapy in order to get the patient into remission. The one-week hospital stay is to monitor the chemo drugs they use and judge the patient's compatibility to them. It usually takes ten to twelve weeks to achieve the remission, but they monitor the response during that week to be sure the drugs are tolerated.

It was such an overwhelming day that my baby was exhausted and we got her settled in and she went right to sleep. We headed home to tell the family. Unfortunately, when my baby awoke later and they started jabbing her, she started crying and did not stop. By the time we arrived the next day it was already decided that she was to go home because the crying was more harmful than helpful. We were going to have to bring her in every day for a while.

Truth Takes Its First Hit

On the way home the conversation was very small based on the life changing information we had received. I had no clue what to say to console my wife or my mind. Was there anything I could have said? If there was, it was not coming to my mind at that time.

Have you ever wondered what it was like to have your soul ripped out of your body while you were conscious? If you are dealing with this, then I'm guessing you do. That is about as close to the truth as I can bring us. We are talking about a three-year-old child and the disease she was handed. For me it would have been easier to stand there and let them perform open-heart surgery while I watched without drugs. I would have preferred that than to see my child suffer.

My wife and I were both so young and naive when it came to this situation. She was twenty-seven and I was thirty. What class in life existed that could prepare us for this new truth?

I knew I needed to curl up in the fetal position and not feel everything I did at that moment. I tried to understand how to help my wife but the reality of what just happened was so overpowering neither of us had a clue what was going on. That silence was deafening.

So many questions, no answers. Not knowing if the doctor lied to us or not to relieve our stress and keep us in the game. So many questions.

BREATHE, JUST BREATHE.

For the moment, that is about all I for one can do.

We shared small talk at best and it was decided that I would break the news to her parents. Neither of us had a clue what had just happened and how it would impact our lives from that day forward. We were still in shell shock. I was trying to find words to use to describe how I felt, to find words to offer comfort to her, not getting words of comfort from her. All this just filled the car with apprehension and fear.

Were we going to lose our child? A question never verbalized but very much in the forefront of our thoughts.

Were we able to handle what we just got handed? I for one did not feel able but as the dad I had to figure out a way. There were no other options. All these questions were running through my head, along with how will I manage under the pressure? Oh yeah, I am a man and I can handle anything.

When we arrived at her parents' house I had already laid it out in my mind as to how I would break the news. As soon as we opened the door, her mom was crying hysterically and out of control. So much for plan A.

The truth took its first hit. What I said was, "We have a problem, but it is manageable." By who or what I had no idea, but surely not them.

Having said that I went into the kitchen where they kept the rum. I poured a small glass and tossed it down. It didn't help. I poured another, still nothing. I was hoping that the rum would transport me out of the pain I was in and help me find some relief.

The ironic part is I did not drink. Not ever. It tasted like crap and I did not feel any better. Why do people do that to themselves on purpose? When you wake up the problem still exists and you feel like shit. Why bother?

We talked for hours and then it was time to go home and call my parents on the West Coast and have this conversation again for the third time in one day.

Trying to have this conversation over the phone was the worst possible way to have it. Speaking the words for the third time and not being able to see their facial feedback, trying to judge their response, not knowing how they were receiving it; do I give them more or less information? This was tearing me up as much as them, again.

I had to relive what I believe was the worst day of my life three times in twenty hours. That day took its toll and I do not think I ever recovered.

Men Don't Speak

My experience over time and paying attention to those around me has taught me that offering a program that is wrapped in a therapeutic umbrella does not work. Society has beaten it into us that men don't talk, don't feel, and, certainly, don't ask for help. Just suck it up and be a man.

So when you offer men one of these programs they usually reply with, "I'm all set with that" or "I'm good" or "I have something really important that night."

You cannot brainwash us to be the protector and provider of the family and handle all things ugly and then expect us to magically reach out for what is offered when that seems to fly in the face of what we know and believe.

The troubling thing to me is that all these fancy places and doctors with all those letters after their names are so out of touch with the male psyche. You can empathize and sympathize until hell freezes over but you will never know the level of pain and despair that runs through that dad in his situation.

We are dads and we make things that go bump in the night go away, except this time there is nothing we can do to fix it, change it, or alter its outcome. That realization takes a huge chunk of your brain that you thought you could use to protect your family and turns it to survival-only thoughts. It only allows you to react to the circumstances as they present themselves without the ability to look ahead and choose a different action based on knowledge and not fear but survival only.

Another thing that torques me up is the large number of therapists and highly educated people that have postulated a theory on how this feels and how to get past it. These are the folks who I describe as theorists. Until you have been told your child has X, whatever life challenging disease, you cannot know the depth of our despair and emptiness, so stop telling us you know how it feels and you have the fix. Really all you have is a theory and I don't give a damn how many letters are after your name.

In my experience all you can do is quiet the mind of outside issues and then hope that the dad can find the courage to delve into his situation and come to terms with it. My personal experience with this issue comes from working with a therapist. He was a nature-based man who respected all living things. He led me and many men I know through a nature-based journey using animals, totems, and the traditions of indigenous people.

Through this process he was able to assist me in quieting the voices of my family of origin, the world in which I absorbed information that was not exactly true, at least as it pertained to me. He introduced many thought options that helped me shake free of all bonds of my past thinking and showed me how to think more freely.

The only thing he could not do was speak to my emptiness and pain as it related to my daughter, although it felt like we were addressing this all along.

The day my daughter's cancer came back for the fourth time, I found myself in such pain and was totally disillusioned and confused that I just turned around and walked away. I did not say thanks or goodbye or see you later; in my pain and anguish I just walked away and never corresponded again. Not one of my prouder moments in life.

As time passed and I was able to look at my part in the process, I became aware that that pattern of behavior was brought on in this situation by the reoccurring pain of not being able to heal or protect my child. There was no logic to any of it, just reflex action to the pain. I will tell you that I have tried for years to go back and apologize or write a letter to explain myself but could never find the courage to do so. In putting it in this form, I am hoping to meet him and look him in the eye and apologize for my actions. I wondered how in hell this pain could still grip me so fully and completely based on all the work I had done.

In my early forties I was on a men's retreat. We were given the task to choose a topic to work on individually over the course of the weekend. In my case I chose to write a letter of goodbye to two friends who were killed in an automobile accident when we were sixteen years old. At sixteen I assure you I had no ability to deal with the enormity of the deaths of my two friends as well as being personally broken from head to toe. I struggled to deal with the survivor's guilt all that time. I tried to come to terms with my feelings and hoped this exercise would ease the emptiness or hollow spot within me.

On this weekend there was a sweat lodge and I was to write the letter and burn it in a ceremony before entering the Inipi (lodge). I went off to the top of the meadow with pencil and paper and my buddy Jake, the dog. I found a comfortable seat and began to ponder what to say while Jake turned a big stick into a little stick.

I sat for what seemed like an eternity and nothing came. I did not realize how closely Jake was watching me as I struggled to put words on paper. Apparently Jake could sense I was stressed and he got up and came over to me and just licked my hand.

JUST? That moment of tenderness caved my world in and I began to cry from my soul. The words flowed and the tears followed suit and on that day I was able to say goodbye to my friends in the darkness and safety of the lodge.

What does this have to do with this book? From sixteen years old to forty-something this had been eating at me and twisting my mind. My take on the connectivity of this event to this story is that the levels of stress that pile up over our life that never get talked about somehow twist our thoughts and warp how we relate in our relationships and to the world.

When something gets stuffed away it festers and finds ways to leak out in the most unwanted ways. I get the fact that this is my story and my circumstance, but how many stories are there that never get talked about and how are they corrupting our ability to communicate or be in a healthy relationship?

What I came to learn was that because of that accident I could not teach my girls to drive, knowing the potential for physical hurt and emotional pain. Once again men don't talk.

Fear

I have never actually looked at fear as an integral part of this equation before, but it played a huge part in my day-to-day living. Not knowing how the disease was going to respond was ever-present, always in the back of my mind, or as far back as possible (never far at all, even now). Every time she got sick or had an ache or pain the first thought was the cancer is back.

This wears on you over the long run and throws a monkey wrench into your decision-making. You want normalcy for your child but you need some for you too. How far do you let go and cheer her on and how much do you cling on and protect? A tight-rope walk at best with no net.

Fear in my day-to-day response to the world was a burden to handle as well. You worry that the people you work with sense a weakness so they may attack you, usually from behind the scenes, wanting your job or your position, undercutting you with the boss, and you find yourself defending, working harder than anyone else in the place. You end up giving up your dignity to maintain your job and the health insurance to protect the family.

Fear is a part of the equation that disallows clear thought as you try to move your family forward at all costs. A little dignity loss here and there takes its toll as well. But that is what I believed I needed to do if it meant providing for the family. I told myself, *Protect the family; you will get over the rest later.*

When you are in the middle of these types of situations and you have been stuffing feelings of anguish deeper and deeper as they come, bouts of rage surface at the worst times. The trigger for me at this time was when my daughter went into our room and found some rolled coins under the bed. Apparently she thought there was enough for everybody and decided to help herself to some candy money. She was around twelve years old at the time and should have known better, but that is not the point.

What I want to discuss is my reaction. Tension must have been high over something during that time and this event triggered me from left field. The utter and complete rage that I unleashed was epic. I was screaming at the top of my lungs and this helpless young lady was sitting there on a kitchen chair, looking up at me with sheer terror in her eyes, surely believing I was going to eat her, head first. Granted, this was an issue that needed conversation but I was gone and out of control, a side effect that comes from shoving everything away, and I can assure you that nothing good came of it because of my involuntary reaction.

Placing the focus on my life like this helps me to see that all the different stresses that came into play at any given time corrupted any chance of clear thought and sound decision making. (Remember this is looking back through a thirty-six year lens.) I was in survival mode most of the time and just reacting to the stimuli that was presented to me.

Being part of something larger than myself, a family, absolutely meant that they had to come first. It was my duty to provide and protect them before myself. Another thought process of the times. I wonder how much of that thought process remains today.

With the divorce rate at fifty-plus percent without a health crisis involved, how unemotionally involved have the latest generations become? The slightest stressor and out the door they go, kids or no kids. Where has accountability gone?

One of the toughest questions I ever asked myself, looking

back after the divorce, was what was my part in the breakdown of the marriage? It is so much easier to point fingers and blame others than to take responsibility for yourself.

The Weight of It All

Depression was an everyday part of my existence. I had no word or any understanding of it while I was in the middle of my experience. It was not until later in therapy that I was finally able to give it a name.

Before that I was just having a shitty day.

It was diagnosed that I suffered from a case of moderate depression. Although there were at least two times that it overwhelmed me to the point that I found myself somewhere other than where I thought I should be and it left me completely unable to function at any level and lasted for at least six hours. I do not know why the six hours stuck with me; perhaps that was all the time I could afford to give it, but each time it was six hours. That rattled me to the core. Out of control, no hope, nowhere to turn. My only thought, "What the fuck do I do now?"

Here is where it (depression) sorts us into categories. We succumb to its pressure, fold our tents, and run away by crawling into a bottle or drugs or an affair, or we decide to begin advocating for ourselves.

This last option is no easy task and feels foreign at first. As we move forward, it starts to lose its grip on our throats and words and thoughts begin to come into our consciousness and *we* become important.

Our needs start to come to the surface and, if we can get back to a whole person status, then we can keep moving forward and do what is necessary for the long haul. This notion may sound like pretty words, but make no mistake: it will raise you to new heights or it will crush you. No in-between. It is do or not do; there is no try (wise word from Yoda).

This is the fork in the road and the decision is on you.

I do not know where this goes in the telling of this story, but here it is. This was happening throughout the time period being discussed. It tells a lot, at least to me.

Money was always an issue. There was always a shortage it seemed. This created pressure in my mind like you cannot understand. I was giving everything I had to work harder and resolve the issue. The situation that this created was this: I *had* to have a Dunkin Donuts coffee and a doughnut every day. That is all I had to hang onto. If I could not do this then I had failed completely.

I had nothing else left.

I know that some shrink is diagnosing me as he/she reads this. I do not want the definition of what that is called; I only know that it was the anchor by which I judged if I was going to make it or not.

Silly perhaps, but in that situation I had no clarity of thought and certainly no one to talk it out with. Arguing with my now ex-wife doesn't count as someone to talk to. I did not understand at the time, so how could I expect her to?

While writing this part my mind flashed back to when I was fourteen and served as the sole provider for my family of six. It was in the summer of my fourteenth year. My dad worked at a steel plant that went on strike. While on strike you do not receive unemployment or anything else. My dad wanted to be a good union man and would not take another job. My mom was not working so it fell to me to go to work and bring in the money to support this family.

Being fourteen you can imagine what work was available. I got a job collecting eggs at a chicken farm. It was filthy, dusty, and backbreaking work. At the end of the week I would come home and give my mom the check I earned so we could at least eat. Perhaps that is where it became engrained in me to be responsible for others.

Neediness

This one crept up on me. I did not realize that there was such a problem until many years down the therapy route when I discovered the name that describes the symptoms.

Being a man in a crisis situation, I automatically relinquished all time and resources to my family. That was what dads were supposed to do. I do not need anything.

But the reality is that we all need something. I needed someone to care for me or about me. I always felt alone in the struggle to provide. I came home from work to a list of more work that needed to be done, never a time to recharge.

Please, I am not saying that wives have it any different or are less overloaded. They are just better at stating the obvious.

We men need to take a lesson and figure how to be heard and wives are the go-to example as far as I am concerned. This has led me to an understanding of the male condition.

The statement that I am about to make is a *quantity* statement not a *quality* statement. My take on this is that we all come into the world with X to give. As long as we give and get back, the giving muscle gets stronger. If, on the other hand, all we do is give and get nothing in return, then we slip into survival mode. We end up having nothing left to give.

I am sure you have all heard of that man that abandoned his family in a time of a health crisis. How easy it is to throw disparaging thoughts his way. But I have come to understand that man and I am inviting him back to this conversation.

- I understand you having to shut down emotionally.
- I understand that you gave everything you had.
- I understand that you are living with a situation that you

have absolutely no control over and it eats at your soul.

- I understand that there are no answers for us as dads.
- I understand that we have been trained not to speak or show any weakness.
- I understand that our families have been trained to look to us for the answer even when there are only questions.
- I understand that we are asked to be Superman in situations that make us feel like a loser because we feel helpless.
- I understand that the possibilities of what can happen to our child leave us hopeless.

I get the whole picture and still I am inviting you back to our table in an effort to reconnect, for your kids and yourself. Your wife may never speak to you again, but your kids need you. You are not alone!

Another thing I have discovered about myself over this time is that I was so needy that any kindness was latched onto and basically sucked dry. A couple of people helped me that way and I am grateful. (You know who you are, thanks.)

The Rock

One of the hardest things to do was handle everyone else's inability to deal with this situation. My perception was that I was forced to be the hard place that they could break against. They could not handle the bad news or the situation, so they dumped it on me.

Like I did not have enough to handle and now I got to handle theirs *and* mine. I told you I am a man and I can handle anything! Well when that bubble burst; I could no longer cope with anything.

In the beginning of this process the treatments were every day for ten days. One week off and we were right back to the schedule, in and out of the city daily.

The financial stress began to raise its ugly head. Gas, parking, and then time out of work meant having to make it up by working the late shift.

The financial stress just added to the unbelievable emotional stress. Later on in the process there were several hospital stays which meant many more trips to visit, along with weekly clinic visits and her pediatrician appointments.

For the first six years we were tied to the hospital. There were few vacations, mostly local camping trips or mill shopping trips, but nothing too far away from the hospital.

We were also just really trying to raise two normal children, so we got them involved in scouts, soccer, and track as a means to keep them stimulated and out of trouble and all that goes with that.

Be very careful dads, I am warning you that horsehair is more addictive than any drug out there. When my youngest daughter was around the age of ten, she discovered horses. Twenty-eight years later she is still heavily involved with them. She paid more for her first horse than I paid for my house and the numbers continue to go up.

I guess I tell this story to point out that it was not all bad, all pressure; it just seems that way.

My oldest got into scouts and went after badges. One year she earned thirty-one badges and her mom made her do everything associated with that badge. Truly focused kids.

Did I mention how proud I am of them? While I am rambling, remember the Cabbage Patch Dolls? They were thirty-five dollars each. Back then that was serious money. My daughters wanted me to purchase a doll for each of them to which I responded, "No; if you want one you will have to figure out a way to earn the money." They collected beer bottles and soda cans and bottles and turned them in. They each purchased three dolls. That is a lot of cans and bottles!

Between the medical needs, my regular work schedule of seven days a week, and working the late shift, it forced me to be out of the house most of the time, so that when I finally did get home I was so tired that I did not want to hear anything but the highlights and only a few of them. My lack of being present to or for my wife created huge pressure between us.

As I said earlier, she took on a load herself and was overburdened too. When you are in the middle of the situation, you cannot see or grasp the enormity of what is happening. I still believed that I could handle everything that was going on until many years into it when the wheels started to weaken and look like they might fall off.

Another incident that came up was around my oldest

daughter when she was fourteen.

When things are going on, things go on. My oldest came home from school with a note from the school nurse saying to bring my daughter to her doctor because they suspected she had a bad case of Scoliosis that went undetected for years because it went front to back, not the usual side to side.

Back to the hospital for verification. Yes, she had it and needed surgery soon. It was serious.

At that particular moment I was between jobs with no health insurance, and this surgery cost thirty thousand dollars. The hospital suggested the Shriners. My wife made the calls and a representative came to our house to discuss the situation. They took into account everything that was going on and said they would do the operation for free.

Thank God for these people!

She had the surgery, had eight vertebrae wired to a steel rod from neck to hip, and came out three inches taller in the end. Have I mentioned that I have difficulty asking for help? Another hit to my ego.

Intimacy

I can hear more than half you guys saying *FINALLY* something I like, *SEX*.

Sorry. That used to be my definition of intimacy as well. In this time frame, watching everyone who was left in my life, there was no one modeling this behavior. It seemed to be *us against them* in some form or another.

Men worked, talked shop, relaxed together, drank, talked politics, hung out, and engaged in sports of some kind.

Women seemed to take care of the kids, house, each other, and did things they enjoyed, like shopping, which is the only example that comes to mind (notice my lack of knowledge here).

Sex is important, but it is only a byproduct of having an equal partnership that shares the good, the bad, and the ugly together.

In certain circumstances one of the partners may be stronger than the other, but as long as it flows back and forth it creates a lasting elastic bond. Having said that, I can tell you I now know what it looks like when I see it in others. If I ever had that, I missed it. I was working. That sounded like a copout, but having no guides I was clueless to develop it. *Just suck it up and be a man* sums it up in my time.

Just in case you are wondering, I do understand what intimacy means and the connotation actually has depth and feeling to it. Holding hands, being strong for each other, having a shoulder to rest your head on when you are bone weary and still feel safe, to snuggle up and just be, to refresh each other and reconnect at the level of soul. When you have this then sharing your bodies is just a natural extension of the connection you have created. For me, seeing this in another couple kicked up jealous reactions.

Upon looking at it, I came to understand that this was missing in my life and I was responsible for my part. Trying not to feel by hiding out in my work just took the possibilities for a deeper connection away.

Others hide out in drinking, drugs, or by having an affair. Regardless, we find ways to hide our feelings of being *less than* because we cannot protect our family the way we believe we should. That feeling is so debilitating and we search for relief any way we can.

When you are not connected with a foundation of equality, the scales seem tilted in one direction or the other. Resentments build and you grow apart over time. Once you pass a certain point, there is no way to repair that which is irrevocably broken. Perhaps we can help each other in the repairs as it pertains to our relationships.

If I knew then what I know now, working on the marriage would and should have been paramount. Friends will come and go, kids will grow and make lives of their own, relationships will start and end, work will continue or not, but in the end if you have not paid attention and made your spouse your number one priority, you will go it alone.

The first thing we can do is look at ourselves in this pressure cooker. How do we get relief? How can we turn down the heat?

The most powerful and destructive tool that keeps us bound to our situation is our ego. The toughest thing to admit is *I* do not know what to do.

Who among us has an answer on how to heal our child? In this instance that little human is my responsibility and he/she has a disease that I am unable to fix or change. Perhaps we need to shift our focus to just being physically and emotionally present for that child, thereby giving him/her the knowledge that he/she is loved and help them to build their connection with their human spirit, one that I can attest to as being the most powerful thing I have ever witnessed. That is a way for us dads who need to fix things to remain in connection with our children, our families, and ourselves.

One of the most important messages I would like to get out here in this attempt to bare all is this: I accept full responsibility for my actions or reactions through this crisis. I blame no one but me. I am angry that there was no one to talk to who may have been able to help smooth the Rocky Mountain-sized problems when they came up by offering facts that would lead to informed decisions.

The way it was/is still needs work. Dads are out here floundering, although it has gotten infinitely better for everyone *except* the dads. We represent at least one third of the unit being treated (mom, child, dad). It is about time we get a little attention too.

If we were, the divorce rate would not be in the eighty-plus percent range. This is meant to shed light on a topic that appears to be buried and needs the light of day.

We can have an impact on this subject by speaking up. Join the talk one of our blogs, www.DuctTapeWontFixThis.com or www.TheMagicHatProject.com, and, if you do not want to speak yourself, perhaps we can create a means to be heard as a whole unit. Either way, if you do not get involved, it will not change. If you do, who knows?

I feel compelled to share my anger that has gone

unrecognized or uncared about for all these years. Having to deal with it alone I recognize that it could have gone a different way than it has. Fortunately I have been able to channel it into doing something constructive, writing this down and sharing it with the larger unit, you. It could have just as easily taken me down and out, and I could have been miserable for the rest of my life and taken this information to my grave, a very selfish thing to do.

I have heard somewhere that a shared load is a load halved. I hope this inspires you to get involved. You do not have to do what I did; just be part of the conversation. Together we can make a difference.

Clinic Visits

These visits were grueling most of the time. But they had wonderful moments too. The only thing that makes this next statement palatable is that these children do not know any other way. This is and has been their life to date, so they just deal with it.

We (parents) are the ones that screw it up with our concepts. I met some extraordinary little kids that had an impact on me to this day. One little girl in particular stole my heart. I will not give her name, but she was truly amazing to watch and interact with. She had Down's syndrome and Leukemia. She was all smiles all the time and was bubbly and outgoing and you just could not ignore her. She could not hold a conversation but she could say, "Kitty, kitty, kitty," and she loved attention. So we found any book in the clinic that had a picture of a kitty and she just beamed as she said, "Kitty, kitty, kitty."

I had not thought of that in a long time. That for me is a very pleasant memory plucked from very dismal circumstances. The grueling parts were the impatient parents who did not want to wait their turn or the emotionally wrecked who just cried along with the crying kids.

Then there were all the staffers and doctors and nurses asking the same questions over and over every week. "Has anything changed in your child's behavior or has he or she been sick?" To which I would have liked to respond, "YES! But it was from the poison you fed her calling it medicine." Sometimes I think the drugs were worse than the disease. Having said that, it begs the question of how I could be there for someone else's precious child and still struggle with being there for my very own precious little girl. The only answer that comes is the difference between being a parent versus a grandparent now that I am one. One you have complete responsibility for, and the next is all you have to do is love them where and how they are, and they love you back unconditionally. A respite in the midst of the chaos that was clinic and having a sick child who had to be there.

The clinic was always a long wait. Everyone had to be there by 9:00 a.m. but we were not seen until between 1:00 p.m. and 3:00 p.m. A day at the hospital was worse than two days of hard labor. I would have actually preferred the hard labor.

Even though the children were familiar with being in this setting, it did not mean that they liked it or did not cry and make for unpleasant circumstances.

It was always a huge load of stress and I emerged washed out, both physically and emotionally, every time. Being in those circumstances tired me out in ways and in places that I did not understand. It happened at a level that I was not in touch with, the soul. I would come away bone tired every time, and I think that being with so many small helpless children worked me over even more.

There were several hospitalizations in the beginning and those were the worst. Being present when a child lost his or her battle was an in-your-face reminder of just how tenuous the battle we were fighting was.

How almost transparent the veil between life and death can be. One minute they were there and the next gone. Where did they go?

We could still see the container that we identified as child but the essence was gone. We had to witness this four times. It leaves a hole in you that nothing can fill, whether it is your child or not. All you can do is hold that parent while actually holding on for yourself.

Through all of this, I held on to the cuter moments as best I could. This is one of those memories:

In the beginning we were told to prepare our child for the complete loss of her hair. Mom started to work on this by telling our daughter that the medicine was going to make her lose her hair. To make this better Mom told her that she would make her pretty hats. Finally the day arrived and her hair started to fall out in big clumps, but then it stopped. She was the one in one hundred who did not lose her hair. We, the parents, thought that was magnificent but she, the child, started to cry. When asked why she said that now Mom was not going to make her pretty hats. This is where a child's priorities become a parent's focus.

Mom made the hats, I promise.

Personal Loss

Someone asked me in passing, "What did you lose along the way?" This is another of those subjects that in your subconscious is just over there, barely out of sight. When you shine the light in that corner, you come to understand that yes, there have been losses. I will try to list them.

Trust. When you are beginning this journey, people start acting very differently and just go away while you are adjusting to this new reality. When you finally come up for a breath and look around and find the landscape a lot less populated with people you thought you could trust, it leaves holes that you are unable to explain, never mind understand. These were the people you trusted and thought were your friends and family and you thought you could count on them to be there.

Faith. In people, in God, in myself. When you lose your ability to believe in something, no matter what that something is, it disrupts how you move forward in life. Your beliefs are shaken and you find yourself reeling, trying to get a new base under you so you are able to have a footing to push off of while you readjust to this new reality. There is never a time to grieve these losses because you are in frantic mode and the road ahead is uncharted.

Family. In the broadest sense of the word, I lost my family. I was so intent on providing for their physical needs that I never addressed their emotional needs. Now I am looked upon as the old man who has nothing of importance to offer now that they are grown and living life on their own.

The other thing I lost was large parts of my life. Long stretches of surviving but not thriving. Would I do it again? Without hesitation. Except I would try to find a balance on how to do it with a different outcome in mind.

My wife. Trying to make some good out of what has happened several years into the situation, my ex-wife and I decided that we would not fight because we had two daughters and three granddaughters and we both loved them. We are friendly and are together with the kids and grandkids on holidays. I still steal the good bits off her plate and she still stabs me with her fork.

Her mom and I have gone at it forever and I still aggravate her even in her weakened condition. Her mom suffers from dementia and does not even recognize her own daughter at different points in time. She will be quiet for a long period, which usually means she is not present or part of what is going on. I still torment her and out of nowhere she leans over and says to me, "Russell, you bastard." She still remembers me and I still love the old bat.

My kids. My younger daughter and I have a *holiday/birthday be nice* relationship. I do not feel welcome in her home and she does not include me in her life. Most of what I know about her I read on Facebook or gather from the occasional eavesdropped conversation. She uses sarcasm as her main means of communication. She is a master at it and anyone who wanders onto her dislike-side comes away sliced and diced, just like the definition of sarcasm equals the tearing of flesh.

My older daughter has three daughters of her own. My granddaughters have Grampa exactly where they want me, wrapped around their fingers. I do as told, when told, and I love it (within reason, of course). Around this daughter I feel tolerated; I know she wants a good grandparent association for the kids.

I want to go on record here that I do not know of any person on this planet who is as strong as my younger daughter. To have stood the test of this disease as many times is truly courageous. I absolutely love her attitude about cancer: If you are going to take me, then come get me, because I'm not going easily. And she lives it daily.

Her sister is second strongest. Along with raising three girls, she and her sister are joined at the hip. You mess with one, you'd better watch out because you get two. A true force to be feared. It is all nice until you cross with either one.

I would like to briefly illustrate this strength in the context of my story. In the beginning of treatment, the hospital kept saying to bring in any siblings, cousins, or friends. This was to show them that what was going on was not fun. They could observe her as she received medical treatment so there would be no jealousy that she was getting something they were not.

On a Saturday, my older daughter was coming in with us. As we drove by a particular church my oldest said to her mom, "Mom, remember when I got my shot in that church and I didn't cry?" Well let me tell you, from that day forward her younger sister never cried again when poked. No matter what they did, bone marrow test, spinal tap, flu shot, nothing. A side note here, sometimes they would miss the first time doing a bone marrow test and have to do it over. What I told my baby was if they missed again we would put them on the table and do it to them. I said it in a way that everyone in the room knew I was not kidding. Those tests were brutal. If her big sister did not cry, then no way was she going to. Her competitiveness started early and has come forth in every aspect of her life.

A cute scenario occurred one trip in. It was on a Monday and the day before I had been helping Grampa with the application of some stain on the trim of his house. As I was wiping it off of one piece, I got a splinter that went through my entire palm, left to right. As my daughter was starting to receive her shots I teased her not to cry like Dad did yesterday with that big splinter. The doctor turned around and said, "Let me see that." She then looked up at me and said, "When was your last tetanus shot?" I could not remember so she told my daughter I was getting a shot today too. When the doctor left the room, I asked my daughter if I had to be brave too and she told me, "Run away, Dad, it hurts." Out of the mouths of babes.

Another side note here. This no crying rings true in my ears. Being brought up as a son, it was pounded into me that men do not cry. Perhaps that was the comfort factor in that scenario that I connected with so well. Looking back, I remember I did not cry until I was forty-two years old. The pressure built up to the point that I could not stand it any longer and something had to give. I remember I was in the kitchen and I leaned back against the counter and knew I was going to die because I was about to cry.

As a man, unthinkable. One tear fell before I stopped it. Oh my God, a chink in the armor. All I remember about that day was whatever was happening caused my insecurities to rear up and howl. I felt abandoned, overwhelmed, out of control, alone, used up, spent, and useless. Not a good or safe place for a man to be. I am not sure how, but I made it.

Society vs. Men

What if this whole thing could be made to be palatable? What if this whole thing did not need to sap everything from you as you try to negotiate these untenable circumstances?

I look around me at the programs that are helping the masses like Alcoholics Anonymous, creating people-based connections. I see it work for hundreds of men and women nationwide, worldwide. I wonder why not us as men in crisis?

I can still hear the cry of the manly men, "I don't need no stinking help!" Those used to be my thoughts as well.

When I look back from this end of my life, I wonder what it would have been like to have genuine help as I transitioned through these circumstances, not having to guess my way through situations that I am woefully inadequate to handle, not making all the missteps and having to go back and start again, a little further back each time. Now it is almost too late to catch up. I can no longer work seven days and some nights, so what does that mean? Am I to remain isolated in my life knowing that I did everything I could think of only to fall short of the mark again?

Overall this has been a very lonely journey. I do not wish this for you. You need to ask yourself a question: If I don't reach out for an assist now, where will I be in twenty years? Sit with that thought and mull it over. Are you sure that will be the outcome that serves your best interest?

If I had the opportunity to do it over, how would I change the experience? I would seek out other men that had been or are in my position. I would ask for help. I needed to not be alone in my decision-making; I needed facts to make informed decisions instead of flying by the seat of my pants.

There was no place to find someone to talk to who knew what I was going through, who could speak to the loneliness that being a dad in this situation meant.

When everyone abandons ship because of their fear around the subject of death, who was I to talk to? I could not talk to the women in my life and admit failure and not knowing. What I needed most was connection: the ability to be heard in the midst of the pain and confusion that was my day-to-day existence. I needed someone to help keep my head up and scanning the horizon for opportunities to move myself and my family forward instead of keeping my nose to the grindstone and just existing in motion. I confused motion with fixing the problems.

Although I am removed from the day-to-day responsibility of caring for my child, it does not remove any of the feelings that are associated with the reoccurrences of the cancer that have happened five more times over the years.

The knowledge that imbedded itself in my psyche from that first diagnosis remains. Each time it returns I am pulled right back into the pit of emotions and relive the worst day of my life again.

I promise you that time did not heal a damn thing. It just revived that helplessness of being dad and having no ability to protect my child.

Although she had her mom and big sister to help her through, as well as all her friends, I on the other hand had no one to talk to. I relived the worst day of my life alone, again and again and again and again and again.

In my heart of hearts I truly believe that my family does not imagine that this had any effect on me at all. How could they know when I had to hide it all this time?

No wonder I am alone at this end of my life. The last occurrence of the cancer happened just two years ago. The latest refresher in the feelings department in case I had forgotten. I hadn't.

Over the years, my being physically and emotionally absent from my family forced them to reach out to others to have those needs met. The reason I was absent was I had no means of coping with the facts of my child's condition and certainly no ability to fix any part of it. The only thing I could do was work. It was the only thing I felt I could control. The rest of that story is in the text elsewhere. I made my decision and was trying to live up to my end, moving us forward to try to beat the odds. That was the only thing I could think to do. It was also an excuse for me not to feel and it provided an escape from that which I could not fix.

The analogy that comes up is it is like being an alcoholic. Once the trust is broken, there is no amount of recovery that is believed, and the only ones that benefit from all this new hope are others. Taking responsibility to look at your missteps and screw-ups goes unnoticed by those who you care about the most. Your family is unable or unwilling to take the chance on you, and so strangers receive the benefit of your growth. It is others who recognize the person that you have become and welcome your assistance.

My outreach has gone to hospice work, working with kids who have cancer and kids whose parent or grandparent has cancer. I also volunteer time at a horse rescue farm doing minor carpentry, yard work, shoveling *stuff*, stacking hay bales. Whatever is needed. As I said earlier, this has been a lonely journey.

Let us stop here and go back for a bit. Life hands you lessons to be learned. Sometimes you learn them the first time, sometimes you need a few more tries.

Supporting my family was a huge undertaking for me at that early age of fourteen. I was proud that I could have that kind of effect in the lives of other people. I certainly did not understand the consequences of learning things out of sequence.

Taking on that lesson that early twisted my thinking when it came to how I thought about my own importance in the scheme of things. As I moved forward, I brought that lesson and many more into the marriage relationship.

Until my daughter was diagnosed, we lived a pretty normal existence of give and take. When the diagnosis came, I automatically took on old habits and took on more than I could reasonably chew.

No matter: I know this pressure and I know what to do. I can do anything, even this.

I guess the universe had some more lessons that it needed to teach me. First, finding my tolerance for pain, then unlearning that which I had learned out of sync and relearning the proper way. Never an easy way to do anything.

I am not sure a woman can relate to the feelings of isolation imposed on us as men any more than we can relate to their imposed rules or regulations. The story of how you act according to the birth order stands the test for me too. I am the oldest of four and have always been the more serious, take-responsibility type of person.

The Impact

Looking back over the years that this unfolded in my life is daunting. Not the big stuff; I can spew that out by rote memory. But the small stuff. Things like how this new level of stress and my lack of knowledge infiltrated my decisions. How this same stress impacted every corner of my being and all areas of my life.

Understand, what I say now is filtered through a thirty-six-year-long lens. I am no super dad that did this in the moment that it needed to be done. What I am saying is that I wish I had been this aware in the moment that it was happening so I would not have guessed, and guessed wrong more often than not. I give you that hindsight is always better, but sometimes that is the only way to make sense of what happened and to clearly see and understand how this under-the-gun decision-making infiltrated everything.

For example, the decision that my wife would have to take on the caring for the kids. To handle the emotional stuff around the sickness and help them grow. At that point of my life I was in no position to allow myself to feel the emotions that were glaringly in my face on a moment-to-moment scale. I had been trained not to feel, not to say I don't know or I need help.

If anything, this was surely the time to suck it up and be a man, whatever that means. If I allowed myself to feel, it would be over. I'd be useless to my family, my life, and myself. My take on it was that she took on that which I could not do and, in my eyes, she got the short end of the stick.

From that decision I strapped on everything else. For me to ask her for help or to do more would tip the scales out of balance. That and I had absolutely no ability to feel at that level. I was still sure my child was in huge trouble. That decision virtually isolated me from the only help that was available. I have stated that friends and family bailed out, so I was just alone. Or I felt alone. But I am a man and I can do anything, figure anything out. I do not need help. Watch me. Another thought that came back and bit my ass, *often*.

Have you ever taken the time to observe how many people watch others and do as they do, never questioning whether or not it was right for their own circumstances? Just do it; plenty of time later to try to undo it and straighten it out. Hopefully not so disastrous that it crippled you financially.

That was the case for me. The only problem was that the people I tried to emulate did not have a clue either. We were all guessing. Even the folks I looked to for guidance were guessing, and they did not have a crisis in their lives and still they screwed up.

Another issue was watching the decisions that I made financially impact my family. Ten or twelve years into this process I was pretty well beaten up emotionally and I made some bad decisions about jobs. I went to work with family, never a good idea, and I took jobs with small companies thinking I was going to make a difference only to fall short again. I will tell you that I took on more work to make up for my screw-ups, often working seven days and two to three nights a week. If I did not have work planned for Sunday, the stress gave me a migraine and I was done for the day, total darkness and quiet. No family time again. I couldn't cope with the reality of what was there.

The circumstances guided me toward jobs that had long hours and low pay but gave me the flexible hours I needed, just in case, and I was super responsible at all of them. First in, last out. Taking on more responsibility than I was ever paid for. Trying to fit in as some kind of normal person.

The least appropriate word for anything in my life was normal. When I'd get home, I didn't have the capacity to hear the day-to-day events that to my family were their crises. I was spent and this created huge amounts of stress between my then wife and me. I did not know her day-to-day struggle and I did not share mine. I just tried to keep us moving forward, again. It all became a blur.

Are you starting to pick up a theme here? I threw myself into work. Surely that proved how much I loved my family. Toward the end they tried to tell me that they did not want things, they wanted me. That couldn't be true. If they really knew me, they would surely want someone else. I was just a hollow shell trying to survive while being responsible for their wellbeing. Surely they didn't know what they were asking.

An analogy that came to mind was that I was like a stuffed animal with all the stuffing emptied out and that shell was spray painted to form a hard surface for others to break against. I continued to work extensively.

Adding to the mix, I had to get them where they needed to be when they needed to be there. My ex-wife did not drive, so that was part of my responsibility as well. She took driving lessons a couple of times, but each time someone almost caused an accident and she gave up.

Please do not get me wrong, my ex-wife busted her butt with a thousand things as well, but this is about my experience. Thirty-six years into this, I can look you in the eye and tell you that in all those years not one person ever asked me how I was doing. Yeah, you get the polite cursory question from a friend or acquaintance, but if you responded with the truth, scratch another name off the Christmas list.

I am part of that eighty-plus percent. The situation became untenable toward the end. Tension was high, hope was pretty well gone, and one day my wife asked me to leave. I fought that for months. I committed to forever and *this* would be a life failure. On top of all I carried inside me this was just too much.

Being unable to fix my daughter, provide better for my family, to have anything in my life that was mine that proved how hard I worked, never once being validated in any way, now being asked to leave was the last straw. At this point I could not have been lower on the emotional scale if I had tried. Everything I held of value was crumbling before my eyes. I was so out of control that I could not even eat. I barely found the courage to exist.

Finally I gave up. I found a room with a friend of a friend and left the house. My youngest was eighteen and just graduating high school. She came home with some friends just as I loaded the truck and she left immediately in tears. I feel that she blamed me for the breakup and never forgave me. I was not allowed at any of her college soccer games or track meets after being present for every one prior to leaving the home. I tried to understand their point of view but was barely surviving and could not accept any more pressure. I had to just try to keep moving, forward or backward, just motion, just survive for the time.

Further Failure

The marriage ended at twenty-seven years. Another failure as a man I had to deal with. I went into such a deep depression that I could not work for over a year. Going from a workaholic to a bum was another blow to my beaten ego. I fell into debt with credit cards and friends. I felt like such a loser. Working my way back from this took as much as I had and then some.

I have lived with this problem that I have no control over for thirty-six years. I will tell you that for the longest time I dealt with this by myself. As time and pressure built, I had to reach out for help, even if I appeared to be weak. I did therapy of one sort or another for fifteen years, trying to find out why I could not get my head around the enormity of this problem. I am a man and I should be able to figure this out. What actually happened was the work we did quieted the lessons learned in the past and allowed me to go inside and find my truth as it is, not as I wish it were. This realization happened later in the process.

When my child's cancer came back for the third or fourth time, I joined a cancer support group trying to figure out what to do, how to feel. Surely they could tell me how to fix this.

The people in this group were either dealing with cancer themselves or they were family of someone dealing with it. I was basically frantic to get a fix for my problem (my daughter's cancer) so I just opened up and spilled my guts in anticipation of getting the answer. They basically let me flop around and expend myself and then, with gentle silk gloves, pulled me back into reality and told me that there was nothing I could do in this circumstance to fix the problem. Just love your child. Period.

This turned out to be my introduction to hospice work. I was able to articulate my fears and misgivings well enough that I was able to establish a strong level of trust with those who were suffering with cancer. From that trust they felt comfortable enough with me that they asked for my help when it came to the end of their journey.

I was never so honored or scared because this forced me to look at my own fears around death. And let us be real here, too. Did I think I might have an influence in fixing it (changing the outcome)? The first time, yes. A hard lesson learned under pressure.

Having had the absolute privilege of aiding eight people on the last leg of this life journey was an ongoing life lesson plan for this man, and the most important lesson that I learned was to show up and be both physically and emotionally present and have no agenda.

That is the lesson I would like to get out to all the people who know someone who is going through a struggle with health. Deal with your stuff elsewhere and just be present for that person. It is not about you. The person will dictate what is important, but mostly they want to talk about what has always been important to them. Let them steer the conversation. When something *needs* to be said, they will say it; just be present to hear it. That statement is unbelievably hard when it is your loved one, but it is still true.

Oh, by the way, they are going to handle this like they handled everything else in their lives. They do not care how you would handle it. This is about them and they have their own ways, so do not try to change them at this late date. Save some unneeded anxiety and pressure and just do it their way.

From there I started working with kids who had cancer and

from there kids whose parent or grandparent had cancer, trying to help them have a voice in the conversation.

I know that I keep talking about cancer. That is where my experience lies. This same information translates to any one of the thirty-two other chronic illnesses that exist, as well as it is just good common sense. My reason for explaining this is to tell you that my ideas are not derived from a book. Everything I say comes from having lived it for an extended period of time, not theories.

Unconditional Love

My father-in-law was my wife's stepdad. Having said that, I would like to say that he was *the* grandparent in my kids' lives. When my daughter was about three or so we were visiting again, and Grampa was having a beer in his favorite chair. Now his chair was kind of out in the room where you could actually walk around it and there was a table to the right. He would set his beer on the table between swigs. Little did I know my youngest was sneaking up behind Grampa and stealing his beer and taking a drink and setting it down and running away giggling while Grampa put up such a fuss that his beer was missing.

Moving forward to shortly after the diagnosis, we went for a visit. As we watched the football game, I noticed he had not had a beer that day. I asked if he forgot to go to the liquor store and he said, "I stopped drinking because I am not going to be the one to tell her, 'No.'" He never drank again.

Another time we were visiting and the girls had their bikes and were riding around the sandy driveway, between Grampa's brand new truck and Nana's almost new car. Suddenly we heard a large crash and ran to see what had happened. My youngest had slipped and absolutely caved in the passenger door of the truck. I was about to have a heart attack and to go off when Grampa stepped in and said, "No problem. I can fix that in twenty minutes. Go ride lower in the driveway." He went in and got his Phillips screwdriver and proceeded to take off the inside of the door and push it out, announcing, "SEE!" Only the forgiveness of a Grampa could pull that off.

Some years later Grampa was diagnosed with cancer. The bond between them was unbreakable. They would sit together and compare notes about how a particular drug affected them as they both had some of the same meds. They compared hospitals, doctors and nurses. They would talk about how different foods affected them.

The one story that sticks out in my mind is about celery. Each of them could eat raw bunches but the smell of it cooking would nauseate them. A wonderful side effect of chemo. They were quite a team.

This same Grampa taught my girls how to drive. I was too busy working.

He was also a World War II Veteran. As hard-shelled as you can get. He could do anything and I watched him take some pretty ugly injuries. Once we were finishing a roof as it was getting dark. All of a sudden we heard, "Ouch!" A huge cry of pain from this guy. We ran over to see what had happened. Rushing to finish, he was using a dull blade in his razor knife and it slipped and cut through the fingernail on his thumb down to the bone. Thinking we were doing a rush job to the hospital, he waved us off and put two Band-Aids on it and finished the job. I probably would have jumped off the roof in pain.

Yet he was putty in my children's hands. I guess unconditional love tames the beast. A lesson I am learning now that I am a grandparent, a lesson unavailable to me in those circumstances. When you are removed from the day-to-day responsibilities of raising kids and not having to say "no" all the time, it relieves the stress and you get to love and be loved unconditionally.

I too find that to be the case with my granddaughters, a whole new experience in my life. I get to watch them be children and not pay attention to their parents and screw up what they were just told, and Mom or Dad look incredulous as to the inability to follow directions. Grampa gets to sit and laugh, just loud enough for my daughter to hear while she gives me the look of daggers asking me if I am having a good time. I just smile. Payback.

When it came to my in-laws I hit the jackpot. Both were very supportive and helpful up to now and I had no reason to believe that would change. What I had no way of calculating was the effect it would have on them. Being grampa or nana has a whole different connotation to it. The stress it put on them was more than they were able to take, although they tried. The relationship changed. In some cases for the better and, in some cases, not so much. Especially when it came to the facts of what was going on. The less they knew the better. Just the highlights were enough and that kept them in the game at a comfort level they could handle. Although they never asked more than their comfort level, I know they could feel the tension as things came up and we stayed away so as not to upset them. This realization just became apparent to me as I am now a grampa and my relationship with my grandchildren has helped me to understand the differences between the two roles.

This was the beginning of the distortion of the truth. Where your beliefs mix with this new reality and you develop new strategies to deal with the situation. These new beliefs that appear to be forced on you begin to weave their way into the decision-making process in all corners of your life. It is like slow poison in your system that you do not recognize for what it is and what it is doing, but it infiltrates every area of your life.

Perhaps part of this story line has triggered you to relate to those feelings in your own life and may force you to ask yourself questions. Please take a moment and sit with it; do not be afraid to just look at it. If we find the courage or the limit of our pain tolerance now, is that not payoff enough to actually do something different than what we usually do? I believe it is said that the definition of insanity is doing the same thing over and over and expecting different results. Would we not all be better off if we could learn by someone else's mistakes or learn from their experiences?

A Goal

Hindsight lets us look at past events and try to understand them with the new information we have gained as we move forward in life. One set of circumstances that I have come to look at is how I changed the way I thought and acted during stressful circumstances, believing that what I did at the time of diagnosis altered the way I thought I was supposed to act moving forward.

I immediately dropped into survival mode, trying to beat the odds that I believed were against us, changing how things were done before quickly became the new norm or habit. These new habits were not as beneficial as I thought, but as life quickly moves ahead you have so much on your plate that you do not go back and readjust them to fit current circumstances. They become the norm.

As I moved forward, I did not readjust to the new circumstances and virtually fell behind in the things that need long-range attention. Things like retirement, investments for the future, life insurance, long-term life needs. At this end of my life I am supposed to retire. That ain't happening. Do you suppose that this is important to talk about with others who have gone down the road ahead of you? No matter what happens, life moves inexorably forward with or without you being present and directing its outcome. It is on you to prepare.

All this begs the question, what am I doing to survive? I had to make some hard and not so hard decisions. Will I ever ask you, "Do you want fries with that?" or say "Welcome to Wal-Mart"? Let's just say those aren't in my plan. So do I crumble into the fetal position and give up? I don't think so! So what can I do? I can hunker down and decide what I have to offer to the world.

1. I can think.

2. I can communicate.

3. I am not afraid of looking inward at myself.

4. Upon reflection I truly do have something of value to offer to my fellow men as well as the world.

5. I can write sort of legibly.

6. I can offer a hand up where none was available for me.

7. I have surrounded myself with upbeat, positive people who see what I have to offer and they believe in me.

8. I believe in my heart of hearts that this is worthy of being brought out into the light.

9. I may move slower than I once did, but I am not dead yet. So please someone tell me I can't do this; that is when my juices start to flow and I get going!

Health Care Practitioners

What can we expect in the way of assistance? The health care industry does not even acknowledge that there is a problem. I believe that, as the problem starts to open eyes and conversation, things will begin to change over time. I do not think we have that much more time to devote to this without taking action.

Sometimes the only way to affect change is to become that change ourselves. I can attest to thirty-six years of same-old, same-old and nothing has been done. I asked a group of five hundred social workers what they thought of my idea and they said it was needed more than I knew. So while we raise awareness of the problem by joining together, that will create a need in their minds and they will figure out a way to develop programs to help dads in the future.

In the meantime I suggest we come together and figure it out ourselves. We set the tone of what works and what standard of conduct we need as men in this situation. Our wives, friends, and family have no idea what to do, so it falls to us to figure it out.

I do not believe for a moment that we are not able to offer each other help, especially in these circumstances. Who knows this heartache and emptiness better than someone who has lived it? There are no theories here, not just ideas in a book. This is based on facts we have lived; we have in-the-field experience.

Will it be easy to break the stereotypes that we have been using as our guides? Hell no. It is ingrained in us. We need to come together in a spirit of cooperation and not one of competition. The lie that we have been fed as men is that everyone is out to screw you.

I strongly believe that a therapeutic answer is not what we

need, though it can be helpful for some. What we need is for other men who have lived the problem firsthand to step up and start helping those coming behind us.

My experience with helping others is that you get ten times more in return for your efforts than by any other means. Besides, you probably do not have all the answers you need either, so this is a win-win situation as we help each other understand the intricacies of dealing with and healing our own issues.

I feel like I should throw in an F-bomb here just to keep it manly.

Please understand, I am not looking to sit around the campfire and sing Kumbaya and talk about our feelings. I personally have been in varying degrees of emotional pain most of my life. I have tried to talk to therapists and other men and was never able to reach into the depths where the pain resided. They have not lived it and cannot reach any level of understanding that is meaningful enough to be helpful to me.

I need another dad who has lived my fears and can relate at a level that touches where I am. Dads coming together to heal themselves are the salvation of their families as we move into the future.

I hope that as men you will look at this from a higher perspective. I have used words like issues, healing, emotional pain, getting help, assistance. We generally associate these with the opposite sex. That is bullshit. If we continue to do what we have always done, what change do you see coming our way?

Another F-bomb seems to be needed here just to keep it manly. Shall I spit and scratch something too? What the fuck? There, are we back on track?

This problem is the elephant sitting in the middle of our

lives, not just the room. We ditz and dance all around it, but it is still in the way of living life as a whole person. The harder we try to push it down, the more it finds places to leak out and disrupt our lives in new and different ways. We need to name it and tame it and move beyond it. Without your help and mine this will not happen. No one else will step up and fix this for us.

Quotes
&
Why They Appear Here

Pause for Reflection

We cannot live our lives alone. Our lives are connected by a
thousand invisible threads, and along these sympathetic fibers,
our actions run as causes and return to us as results.
-Herman Melville

I believe there is a reason why this saying has entered my life. There are thirty-two million dads who have a similar situation as mine, and I have been tasked to try to build a bridge to connect us.

Who am I to build a bridge? How am I to build a bridge? Questions that derail most dreams, almost did mine too. However, having lived this nightmare existence for more than half my life, I had to decide if I was going to allow it to define who and how I really am. Short argument. Answer, no way in hell. After a failed marriage, failed career direction, my kid hates me, the other one tolerates me, having done this alone and in the dark most of the time, knowing that I have so much experience to offer and other people accept it willingly and appreciate it, this I do for me, period.

Think, think, think. How do I reach out to the people who are in similar circumstances? Does what I have to say have value. Will it make a difference? Could it really help? I had to do the research to be sure before committing time and limited resources. What I found was that the two dreams I had were viable and had the possibility of helping the most people. One is working with the kids affected by these chronic illnesses, and, two, the dads who are affected by them. Now how do I reach these people in their time and space? I started working on the idea around kids. I spent time and money getting that in gear and then was rerouted to work with dads first because I was told by a very large contingent of people working with that target population that the work I was planning for the dads was way more important based on the fact that there was nothing out there for them.

Over five hundred people working directly with this target population from every corner of this country all saying the same thing had an impact on my decision to do this book first in an effort to reach out and start a conversation that has a potential to make a huge difference. The only way I can think of to be heard is to tell my truth.

Is it pretty? No. Will it make men uncomfortable to read this? A resounding yes. But let me ask you, how is your way working? Ask yourselves what great things have come into existence when men put their heads together in a spirit of cooperation and not competition. This is how we build that bridge. Not any one man but a community of men with a purpose can create anything.

Here is my hand, will you join me? I know I cannot do it by myself.

I AM ONLY ONE
BUT STILL I AM ONE
I CANNOT DO EVERYTHING
BUT STILL I CAN DO SOMETHING
AND BECAUSE I CANNOT DO EVERYTHING
I WILL NOT REFUSE TO DO THE SOMETHING I CAN DO
-EDWARD EVERETT HALE

This helps me understand that I deal with the symptoms of disease. It reminds me that things like the environment that our food is grown in or the pollutants that are thrown into our air and dumped into the soil daily that cause these diseases need to be addressed. But that passion is for others. My passion is the dads and families I may be able to offer an assist to. If I can offer even one father a way to transition through the uncertainty of having a child in crisis and help maintain the family unit, then laying myself bare will have been worth it. To relieve the stress of having no one to talk to who understands you where you are. To not end up at the other end of your life alone. These are my hopes.

When you discover your mission, you will feel its demands. It will fill you with enthusiasm and a burning desire to get to work on it.
-W. Clement Stone

My experience of this mission is I had to push like hell until it achieved motion and now it pulls me along. While I am explaining my idea to people, they ask thought-provoking questions, offer their perspectives, offer their help in any way they can. They just want to be involved with a good idea. This is that good idea. That motivates me daily and my days usually start at three or four in the morning and end when I collapse at night only to start fresh same time tomorrow. I tell you this with no hesitation: I am sixty-six years old and I have never felt this alive in my entire life. This project I do for others, which makes me a part of something larger than myself. It lifts me up to see over all those distractions that kept my head down trying to figure out how to simply survive. To flourish you need to keep your feet on the ground and your head in the air seeing all the opportunities that exist just for the taking. Know this, Dads: there are things in the works for you to help your child. To stay updated, to remain connected to this community, to help you stay connected to your child and your family, please visit our blog.

Adversity introduces a man to himself.
-Author unknown

For me, pain is what moves me. Adversity is the cause. Understanding at my core is the result. But you must be able to listen for the answer. I am a stubborn man who can endure huge amounts of pain, but when the pain is more than my knees will hold up, I have to admit defeat and reach out for help. Therapy helped quell the teachers of the past and allowed me to navigate the present by going deeper inside where my answers and truth lay waiting.

He who has a why to live can bear almost any how.
-Freiderich Nietzsche

This speaks to me at a level I have difficulty sharing in words. Perhaps it stems from my time doing hospice and being present to the human spirit in action. I have seen the human spirit cheat death as with my daughter. I have also seen the person who completely ignored that spirit, who gave up and died unnecessarily from the most treatable form of cancer. We have the most powerful force on earth within us. The trick is to acknowledge it and tap into it. When we do we are unstoppable. Join me for a dip?

Disease can be our spiritual flat tire, disruptions in our lives that seem to be disastrous at the time but end by directing our lives in a meaningful way.
-Bernie S. Siegal

On a personal level, as I stated earlier in this piece, the day my child was diagnosed was the worst day in my life, but I am compelled to make something positive of it which drives me forward daily. I would like to ask a favor of you. It is important to me to keep my family anonymous so I am asking that whenever I say my child or my daughter, you insert your child's name there, boy or girl. That makes this book ours. We are coerced into not speaking by society and that has added such a burden to find relief from all the stressors that go with the responsibility of dealing with a sick child. As men in this situation we need to come together and take back our right to speak and feel and to ask for and receive the help we need to move forward so we are not simply guessing at what to do or how to do it. The first hurdle to be cleared, our ego.

God will never give you more than you can handle.
-Written on a hospital wall

The first time I saw that on the wall, I wanted to hunt the person down and beat him to a pulp. How dare someone tell me what I can handle, even if it be God. At this point I was full of rage and turned away from God. I blamed him for these circumstances and my child's sickness. My thoughts were if this is the best you can do, leave us alone and I will take it from here. My life became very complicated as time passed and many years into it someone handed me the poem about footsteps in the sand. I sat down and cried. Basically the poem says that while looking back over your life, when there was only one set of footprints in the sand, that you were being carried by God, not abandoned and the footprints were not your own.

It is my judgment that you must believe in something bigger than yourself. Call it anything that gives you comfort. Your choice. No right or wrong answer here. If you turn away from everything, as I did, you leave yourself no way out. Who or what can handle your rage other than something larger than life, surely no mere human. When the pressure of dealing with situations so far outside your ability to cope with or even understand starts to overflow, you have to have something to fall back on. I cut those ties and suffered the consequences for longer than I needed to. Did I mention I am stubborn?

A life spent making mistakes is not only more honorable but more useful than a life spent doing nothing.
-George Bernard Shaw

Perhaps I seek forgiveness for all the mistakes I have made. Some of the mistakes I regret the most are being out of the house so much which led to being out of my family's lives and teaching them my bad habits. They learn much more from what you do than by what you say. As far as forgiveness goes, you seek it from outside, but what you really need is to get it from inside. We are harder on ourselves than any outsider could possibly be. If I heard someone talking to another person the way I talked to myself, I would report him to the authorities.

Sometimes in tragedy we find our life's purpose – the eye shed a tear to find its focus.
-Robert Brault

I have fought this project for a long time; I should have embraced it sooner. Fear and truth held me captive - the fear that I would have to put myself out there for public consumption and telling my truth was terrifying at first. Fortunately, if you live long enough, you come to peace with who and how you are. Then the fear of continuing to hold back your truth and your story is more painful than sharing it. Fear of how you will accept my story no longer is strong enough to keep me from telling it. How you accept it is out of my hands, but it is my truth.

Another life lesson I have learned is that we are all more alike than we are different. I ask you to sit with that for a moment and ponder the enormity of that thought. Happiness, sadness, joy, fear, needing to love, needing to be loved, needing to belong to something larger than ourselves. We all experience these at different levels but try to differentiate ourselves by the circumstances we find ourselves in. Trying to justify ourselves. What if we find balance? Would that change anything?

People are resilient. After all every person born has recovered from 9 months on life support.
-Josephine Hart

I just thought this a nice enlightenment.

*Men, like nails, lose their usefulness when they lose direction
and begin to bend.*
-Walter Savage Lander

Loss of direction comes when the weight of responsibility overwhelms even the most devoted man who has lost the concept of self. I would truly like you to stop right here for a moment.

Go back and reread the saying and my take on it.

I want to write a thousand more thoughts here but I am not doing that. I would ask you to write your thoughts about this and share them with me. This was so powerful when I read it that I stopped in my tracks and fell into deep thought about how this described my journey as a man in a crisis situation.

Weekends don't count unless you spend them doing something completely pointless.
-Bill Watterson

Truly a foreign concept to me throughout my life; I spent my time working. As I look back, there was a need to provide for my family, but it was also a means for me to hide from the thoughts about, what if. When I allowed myself to go down that road, it quickly led me to the depths of depression, a place I did not want to go. Being alone in my mind was not a safe place for man nor beast.

Learn all you can from the mistakes of others, you won't have time to make them all yourself.
-Alfred Sheinwold

The reason we make so many mistakes is that there are few, if any, mentors or guides on this path. We are so shackled down by false beliefs that we cannot even speak to each other. As boys we are taught to be competitive from an early age. In school, sports, work, we are not pack animals. We are thought of as at our best when we are producing better than those around us and that is what is celebrated.

Coming together as a community to address the larger picture by sharing knowledge and progressing together as a whole is not. It makes you wonder when are we as men going to take our heads out of our asses and take back our right to be part of the whole? Share the load, the lead. Relieve the pressure a bit and spread the wealth around. By wealth I mean the glory of being a part of something larger than just you and your individual accomplishments. They are nice but you have to be on twenty-four/seven just to keep up the momentum. Is this part of the plan that keeps us under control? When controlled men come together with purpose, they change the world. Will you join me?

Russ's Rants

I am pissed. I have busted my ass all of my life. I never worked any less than sixty hours a week trying to provide for my family. I did not drink, gamble, or chase other women. On top of that, I had to try to keep everyone else together as we transitioned through my child's illness, never having any place to unload my pressure, only to end up with no wife, no home, no retirement, and alone.

How is it that we live to a point in our lives, carrying these burdens alone, that the mind finally says, ENOUGH? Then we cave in to the pressure and decide to do something different, something totally against every belief we held sacred to this point. When we actually stop and look at the information we have been given over time, and realize that we have been duped, or fed misinformation, or handed someone else's twisted view of how the world should be, something snaps. At least for me it did.

As I searched for different information and systems to deal with what and how I handle life's curveballs, I find that I am required to reinvent most of what I believe to be the truth. If you can find the courage to separate yourself from the current group, think and analyze your own circumstances and how they measure up to your expectations, you may find a level of discomfort that forces you to look closer. That is what happened to me. I could no longer function as I had been. Everything I thought I was working for – home, family, future, the proverbial happy ending – *EVAPORATED*.

When this happened to me I chose to start questioning things. What is really happening? Who says that is the way to do things? What is the truth and whose truth is it really? When you take time to look around you at the systems that are in place that govern our lives, I mean really look, you start to get a glimpse of how the deck is stacked against us. The systems I am referring to are schools, city, state and federal government, the environment, our banking and credit systems, all media, the stock market, advertising and corporate practices, chemical companies, agribusiness, and the petrochemical industry. My suggestion is to pick just one of these and dig in deep to raise your own awareness.

The environment is one that lands on my plate with a thud. The careless use of chemicals and disposal of the same create health issues that affect us as humans. They enter our bodies through the food we ingest and the water we drink and the lotions, potions, and pills we take to cure the diseases that are created by these chemicals in our environment.

The chemical companies have gone all over the world and bought up the seed distributors. Then they sprayed the fields of the world with chemicals that killed off any other vegetation so that the soil will only allow their GMO seeds to grow and the crops that result from that chemical soup are then harvested and fed to you and me.

Ask the government: they say it is just fine based on the chemical companies' tests and research. You do not think they would lie, do you? Remember tobacco was good for us too.

Every time you turn around there is a new scent that takes away a house full of rotting food and dirty clothing smells and makes it smell like spring. Then there are the motion activated scent sprayers that shoot sweet smells into the air so you never get the real aroma of your life because you are transported to your favorite garden somewhere else.

We are now paying the price for all the chemicals and compounds we have allowed to enter our lives for which we have been sold a bill of goods as to their causing no harm. In my estimation we have a pandemic on our hands. It is all the variations of chronic illnesses that we currently live with. Fifty years ago cancer was rarely heard of; now one in four is affected. That should be alarming to all of us.

Another thing that has taken a huge hit is the truth. Is there any such thing anymore? The reporting of the news is no longer unbiased or truthful. In the last thirty or so years we have gone from fifty independent news sources down to five. We are being led in a particular direction that is not in our best interest. We are being manipulated and taught not to think for ourselves. Take a look for yourself. What part of a politician's story do you believe? Remember the weapons of mass destruction story? Or the supposed ship attack that started the Viet Nam police action that never happened? Or the health care reform that has never truly come to fruition? Or the welfare reform that slugs along consuming a large portion of our resources? Or the rich politicians giving their friends an extra hand through tax incentives, paid for by you and me, the middle class, supposedly to create jobs and keep America working? In the end, only to find corporate heads shipping jobs overseas to countries that have virtual slave labor as a work force.

We seem to be fed this ongoing line of BS and are expected to fall in line with what is said no matter how ridiculous it sounds or what we know is the truth. We have been fooled by those slick word merchants who have done all the psych studies around how to manipulate the masses into doing what they want them to do, when they want them to do it. We are told that cars get thirty miles per gallon until you buy one and yours only gets seventeen. Then you are told you are the one who is doing something wrong like driving too fast or overloading the vehicle.

How about the banking industry or the Wall Street people, selling us their line of crap? No matter where you look, it is all the same. We the people need to wake up and look around and take stock of just how much we are willing to give away to someone so we can live a sort of comfortable life where we do not have to think for ourselves. That is exactly what they are vying for: just give them (us) enough so they follow along, do not get out of line and, simply, do what they want. We are being manipulated and sold for corporate profit. We the people no longer matter except as to how we can be coerced into consuming the deadly products big business creates.

It starts with the food supply causing all manner of illness, which sends us into the health care system, which feeds us the chemical compounds designed to cure the disease that was caused by other chemicals in the first place. I could go on and on, but I am dealing with another problem in writing this book. Don't even get me started.

About now you are probably asking yourself what does this have to do with why I bought this damn book? Unfortunately, it all ties together. I hit on some of the topics that I believe have a compounding effect on our lives. This is not really the forum to discuss them in depth but just to bring them into the light. They all affect us at some level and we need to look at them as they affect our families' health. We can and must take charge of ourselves before it is too late. We have been waiting for someone else to fix this for us and we can wait no longer. We need to act on our own behalf, NOW.

• • •

I realize that people will read this section and try to discredit me because I have no credentials like Accountant, Scientist, Economist, or whatever. My response is to ask HOW MANY DEGREES DO YOU NEED TO KNOW WHEN SOMETHING IS TOTALLY SCREWED UP?

A Final Word

As the author of this memoir I have read and reread this over and over, making sure it was true and honest. What I have come to understand is that how I write is unlike any other writer I have ever read. What I notice is that I truly am reliving these events as I write about them. What I have come to understand about my writing is that it follows my mind in the way it flows. As I reread this story, my mind jumps from the emotional stress of that event to something light, or at least opposite to the strong feeling event I just talked about. It's almost that if I don't ease the tension of what I just relived, I will not be able to continue. Perhaps it is an effort on my behalf to give the reader as well as myself a break from that we are reliving. None of this is easy but it is definitely necessary.

To tie it all together. This is the story of how the diagnosis of cancer in my child has played out in my life, no one else's. There were four members of my family, and if you asked them to write their version you would probably think it was a totally different family. No matter. What is most important is this: as you look at your family through a new lens, that you have a different wider view to help each other cope in the pressure cooker of your child's diagnosis. There are a large number of chronic illnesses and all affect our kids. I have included a list of the illness so you know this story is not just about cancer; that just happens to be my story.

I am feeling pretty exposed in writing this all down for everyone to read. Guys aren't supposed to feel things and supposedly are strong and nothing bothers us. I hope this helps debunk that theory. It has affected everything in my life.

If I can help just one family stay together by putting my story out there this way, I will consider this a success. Remember, none of us truly knows how to act in these circumstances. Just know it is a pressure cooker for everyone. I will say this again for everyone to reread: Dads need help too.

Some Resources

For those of you who need the info offered by an authoritative voice, I have found some of the most recognizable web sites that we use as "official" followed by a list of chronic illnesses and their own web sites.

Center for Disease Control / CDC Atlanta, Georgia
www.cdc.gov/chronicdiseases/overview
Chronic List Coach
www.chronicillnesscoach.com
American Cancer Society
www.cancer.org

Just CANCER alone in 2014 will have 1,665,540 new cases diagnosed. The corresponding deaths are 585,720. The other stat that blows my mind is that cancer is the cause of death of 1 in 4 in America;THAT'S 25% OF DEATHS IN AMERICA. They even break it down to how many by state.

I believe you are intelligent and capable of reading these stats yourself. I get overwhelmed by these stats and I am hoping that just by bringing some onto your radar that you will pick up and help create change in how we live our lives and make the changes necessary to reverse the downward spiral we appear to be in. Even if the changes mean starting with the leadership of companies, agencies assigned to watch our safety, even the leadership of this country if necessary. When we get angry, things change.

Chronic Illness List

1. Addisons Disease
   www.addisonsdisease/mayoclinic
2. AIDS
   www.AIDS.gov
3. Anemia
   www.anemia.com
4. Ankylosing Spondylitis
   www.ankylosingspondylitis.org
5. Asthma
   www.asthma.com
6. Cancer
   www.acs/cancerfacts&figures2013
7. Celiac Disease
   www.ciliacdisease.net
8. CFIDS
   www.cfids.org
9. Cornary Heart Disease
   www.americanheartassociation.org
10. Crohns Disease
    www.crohnsdisease.net
11. Cystic Fibrosis
    www.cysticfibrosis.com
12. Diabetes, type 1,2.
    www.diabetes.org
13. Ehlers-Danlos syndrome
    www.ehlers-danlossymdrome.com
14. Fibromyalgia
www.fibromyalgia.com

14a. Graves Disease
  www.gravesdisease.com
15. Guillain Barre Syndrome
  www.guillianbarresyndrome.net
16. Hashimoto's Syndrome
  www.hashimotossyndrome.com
17. Headache
  www.headache.org
18. Interstitial cystitis
  www.interstitialcystitis.com
19. Lupus
  www.lupus.org
20. Lyme Disease
  www.lymedisease.org
21. Meniere's Disease
  www.meineresdisease.org
22. Multiple Sclerosis
  www.multiplesclerosisfoundation.org
23. Muscular Dystrophy
  www.musculardystrophy.org
24. Myasthenia Gravis Disease
  www.myastheniagravis.org
25. Osteoarthritis
  www.osteoarthritis.com
26. Parkinsons Disease
  www.parkinsonsdisease.com
27. Reflex Sympathetic Dystrophy
  www.rsdsyndrome.com
28. Rheumatoid Arthritis
  www.rheumatoidarthritis.org

29. Scleroderma
   www.scleroderma.org
30. Sjogranis Syndrome
   www.sjogranissyndrome.org
31. Tay-Sacs Disease
   www.tay-sacsdisease.com
32 .Ulcerative Colitis
   www.ulcerativecolitis.net

I'm sure there are more, that this is an imperfect list. Absence is not meant as a slap in the face; it is just another example of how human I am.

**We look forward to having you
join the conversation at**
www.DuctTapeWontFixThis.com
and at
www.TheMagicHatProject.com

And find us on Facebook at
Duct Tape Won't Fix This
and at
The Magic Hat Project